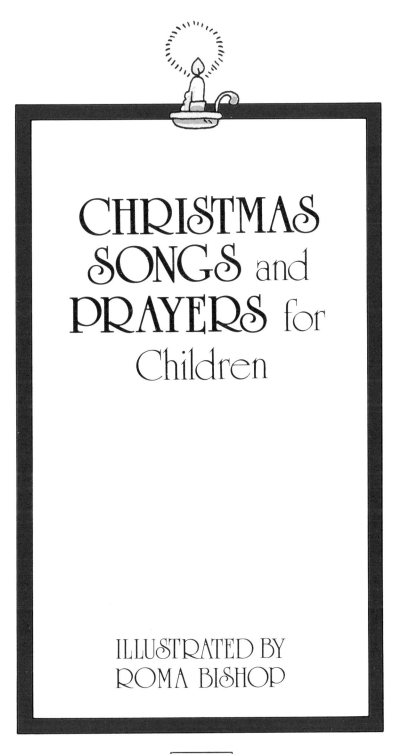

CHRISTMAS SONGS and PRAYERS for Children

ILLUSTRATED BY ROMA BISHOP

SMITHMARK

A Templar Book

This edition published in the USA in 1993 by
SMITHMARK Publishers Inc., 16 East 32nd Street,
New York, NY 10016.

First published in Canada 1993 by
Smithbooks, 113 Merton Street, Toronto, Canada M45 1A8

SMITHMARK books are available for bulk purchase for sales
promotion and premium use. For details write or call the manager of
special sales. SMITHMARK Publishers Inc., 16 East 32nd Street,
New York, NY 10016; (212) 532-6600.

Produced by The Templar Company plc
Pippbrook Mill, London Road
Dorking, Surrey RH4 1JE, Great Britain

ISBN 0-8317-5168-1

Printed and bound by LEGO, Vicenza, Italy

10 9 8 7 6 5 4 3 2 1

This delightfully illustrated collection of Christmas carols and short prayers has been specially compiled for young children. The traditional songs are childhood favorites that tell the story of the nativity. The prayers, many newly composed, have been chosen for small children. They emphasize the special thoughts and feelings of loving and giving that symbolize the special spirit of Christmas.

THE FIRST NOEL

The first Noel the angel did say
Was to certain poor shepherds in fields
as they lay;
In fields where they lay, keeping their sheep,
In a cold winter's night that was so deep:
Noel, Noel, Noel, Noel,
Born is the King of Israel!

They looked up and saw a star,
Shining in the east, beyond them far;
And to the earth it gave great light,
And so it continued both day and night:
Noel, Noel, Noel, Noel,
Born is the King of Israel!

And by the light of that same star,
Three Wise Men came from country far;
To seek for a king was their intent,
And to follow the star wheresoever it went:
Noel, Noel, Noel, Noel,
Born is the King of Israel!

This star drew nigh to the northwest;
O'er Bethlehem it took its rest,
And there it did both stop and stay
Right over the place where Jesus lay:
Noel, Noel, Noel, Noel,
Born is the King of Israel!

Then entered in those Wise Men three,
Fell reverently upon their knee,
And offered there in his presence
Both gold and myrrh and frankincense:
Noel, Noel, Noel, Noel,
Born is the King of Israel!

Then let us all with one accord
Sing praises to our heavenly Lord,
That hath made heaven and earth of naught,
And with his blood mankind hath bought:
Noel, Noel, Noel, Noel,
Born is the King of Israel!

Loving Father help us
we pray,
As we rejoice this
Christmas Day,
To be loving and giving
in every way.

O Father of goodness,
We thank you each one
For happiness,
    healthiness,
Friendship and fun,
For good things we
    think of,
And good things we do,
And all that is
    beautiful,
Loving and true.

Thank you, dear Lord
for sending your only son, Jesus,
to Earth on that Christmas
night so long ago.
Like a loving shepherd,
he watches over us,
protecting us from danger and harm.
Help us to be more like him
so that we can take care
of all your tiny creatures
like Jesus takes care of us.

8

Grant, heavenly Father,
that as we keep the birthday of Jesus,
he may be born again in our hearts,
and that we may grow in the
likeness of the Son of God,
who for our sake was born
son of man; through the
same Jesus Christ our Lord.

Amen.

WHILE SHEPHERDS WATCHED

While shepherds watched
their flocks by night,
All seated on the ground,
The Angel of the Lord came down,
And glory shone around.

'Fear not,' said he (for mighty dread
Had seized their troubled mind);
'Glad tidings of great joy I bring
To you and all mankind.

To you in David's town this day
Is born of David's line
A Savior, who is Christ the Lord;
And this shall be the sign:

The heavenly Babe you there shall find
To human view displayed,
All meanly wrapped in swaddling bands,
And in a manger laid.'

Thus spake the Seraph: and forthwith
Appeared a shining throng
Of angels praising God, who thus
Addressed their joyful song:

'All glory be to God on high,
And on the earth be peace;
Good-will henceforth
from heaven to men
Begin and never cease.'

O lord Jesus, who for
love of us
lay as a baby in a
manger,
we thank you that by
your coming
you brought joy to all
the world.
Help us at this
glad time
to try to make others
happy for your sake.

Jesus Christ, thou
child so wise
bless mine hands and
fill mine eyes,
and bring my soul
to paradise.

You came to Earth,
sweet Jesus
To light the way for me
That I might follow in
your path
And safely come
to thee.

Dear Jesus, it is Christmas.
Your special time, when you
came to Earth to help us all.
Help me to be more like you
and to follow your teachings.
To love everyone, even those
people who are unkind to me.
Help me be kind and generous
not only at Christmas, but
every day of the year.

HARK! THE HERALD ANGELS SING

Hark! the herald Angels sing
Glory to the newborn King;
Peace on earth and mercy mild,
God and sinners reconciled:
Joyful all ye nations rise,
Join the triumph of the skies,
With the angelic host proclaim,
Christ is born in Bethlehem:
Hark! the herald Angels sing
Glory to the newborn King.

Christ, by highest heaven adored,
Christ, the everlasting Lord,
Late in time behold him come
Offspring of the Virgin's womb!
Veiled in flesh the Godhead see,
Hail the incarnate Deity!
Pleased as man with man to dwell,
Jesus, our Emmanuel:
Hark! the herald Angels sing
Glory to the newborn King.

Hail the heaven-born Prince of peace!
Hail the Son of Righteousness!
Light and life to all he brings,
Risen with healing in his wings;
Mild he lays his glory by,
Born that man no more may die,
Born to raise the sons of earth,
Born to give them second birth:
Hark! the herald Angels sing
Glory to the newborn King.

Help us, dear Lord,
to be thankful this
Christmas time for all
the gifts we have
received. Let us not
forget those who are
less fortunate and to
share all that we have
with those in need.

Loving Father,
it's Christmas Day
Please help us in our
work and play.
Teach us to show both
love and care
For other children
everywhere.

O LITTLE TOWN

O little town of Bethlehem,
How still we see thee lie!
Above thy deep and dreamless sleep
The silent stars go by.
Yet in the dark streets shineth
The everlasting light;
The hopes and fears of all the years
Are met in thee to-night.

O morning stars, together
Proclaim the holy birth,
And praises sing to God the King,
And peace to men on earth;
For Christ is born of Mary;
And, gathered all above,
While mortals sleep, the angels keep
Their watch of wondering love.

How silently, how silently,
The wondrous gift is given!
So God imparts to human hearts
The blessings of his heaven.
No ear may hear his coming;
But in this world of sin,
Where meek souls will receive him, still
The dear Christ enters in.

O holy Child of Bethlehem,
Descend to us, we pray;
Cast out our sin, and enter in,
Be born in us to-day.
We hear the Christmas Angels
The great glad tidings tell:
O come to us, abide with us,
Our Lord Emmanuel.

Thank you, God,
for the joys of Christmas:
for the fun of opening
christmas stockings;
for christmas trees
with sparkling lights:
for exciting parties;
for christmas cakes
and cookies;
thank you, God.
Thank you for all the
happiness of Christmas time;
thank you for all
the lovely presents we receive,
but thank you most of all
that Jesus was born
as a baby on the
first Christmas day.
Thank you, God.

Dear baby Jesus, we have come to
find you in the stable at Bethlehem.
May we love you as Mary loved you.
May we serve you as Joseph served you.
May we worship you as the angels
worshipped you, Jesus, our King.

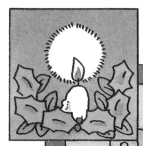

AWAY IN A MANGER

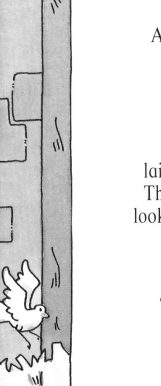

Away in a manger,
no crib for a bed,
The little Lord Jesus
laid down His sweet head.
The stars in the bright sky
looked down where He lay—
The little Lord Jesus
asleep on the hay.

The cattle are lowing,
the Baby awakes,
But little Lord Jesus,
no crying he makes.
I love Thee, Lord Jesus!
look down from the sky,
And stay by my side
until morning is nigh.

Be near me, Lord Jesus;
I ask Thee to stay
Close by me for ever,
and love me, I pray.
Bless all the dear children
in Thy tender care,
And fit us for heaven
to live with Thee there.

Heavenly Father,
thank you for the joys
of winter
For snow and wind,
and sparkling frost;
For cosy fires and
indoor games;
For warm clothes and
shelter of our homes;
On stormy nights; thank
you, heavenly Father.

Christ is born and now lies sleeping,
come and sing your song to him!
Sing, my friends, and make you merry,
Joy and mirth and joy again;
Lo, he lives, the King of Heaven.
Now and evermore. Amen.

SILENT NIGHT, HOLY NIGHT

Silent night, holy night,
all is calm, all is bright,
round yon virgin mother and child;
holy infant so tender and mild:
sleep in heavenly peace,
sleep in heavenly peace.

Silent night, holy night.
Shepherds quake at the sight,
glories stream from heaven afar,
heavenly hosts sing alleluia:
Christ, the Savior is born,
Christ, the Savior is born.

Silent night, holy night.
Son of God, love's pure light
radiant beams from thy holy face,
with the dawn of redeeming grace:
Jesus, Lord, at thy birth,
Jesus, Lord, at thy birth.